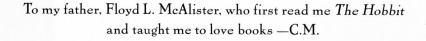

To my father, Floyd L. McAlister, who first read me *The Hobbit*
and taught me to love books —C.M.

For Adam, my Samwise I am glad you are here with me . . .
'til the end of all things. —E.W.

Text copyright © 2017 by Caroline McAlister
Illustrations copyright © 2017 by Eliza Wheeler
Published by Roaring Brook Press
Roaring Brook Press is a division of Holtzbrinck Publishing Holdings Limited Partnership
175 Fifth Avenue, New York, New York 10010
mackids.com

This is an independently created biography of J. R. R. Tolkien and is not
authorized, endorsed, or sponsored by the J. R. R. Tolkien Estate.

Library of Congress Cataloging-in-Publication Data
Names: McAlister, Caroline, 1960– author. | Wheeler, Eliza, illustrator.
Title: John Ronald's dragons : the story of J. R. R. Tolkien / Caroline
    McAlister ; illustrated by Eliza Wheeler.
Description: New York : Roaring Brook Press, 2017.
Identifiers: LCCN 2016024232 | ISBN 9781626720923 (hardback)
Subjects: LCSH: Tolkien, J. R. R. (John Ronald Reuel),
    1892–1973—Biography—Juvenile literature. | Authors, English—Biography—
    Juvenile literature. | BISAC: JUVENILE NONFICTION / Biography &
    Autobiography / Literary. | JUVENILE NONFICTION / Social Science /
    Folklore & Mythology.
Classification: LCC PR6039.O32 Z6954 2017 | DDC 823/.912 [B] —dc23
LC record available at https://lccn.loc.gov/2016024232

Our books may be purchased in bulk for promotional, educational, or business use.
Please contact your local bookseller or the Macmillan Corporate and Premium Sales Department
at (800) 221-7945 ext. 5442 or by e-mail at MacmillanSpecialMarkets@macmillan.com.

First edition 2017
Book design by Andrew Arnold
Printed in China by RR Donnelley Asia Printing Solutions Ltd.,
Dongguan City, Guangdong Province

1 3 5 7 9 10 8 6 4 2

John Ronald's Dragons

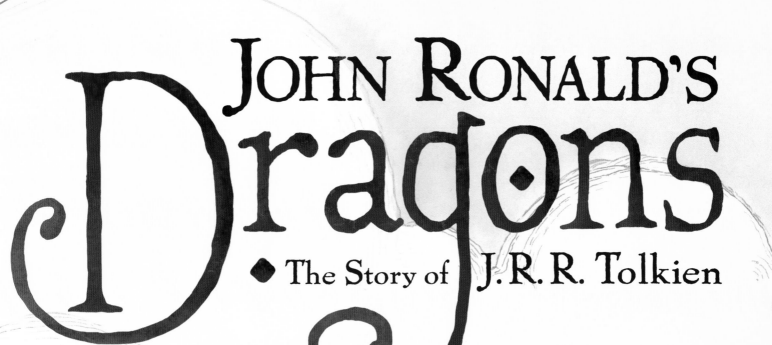

• The Story of J.R.R. Tolkien

Caroline McAlister

Illustrated by
Eliza Wheeler

ROARING BROOK PRESS

New York

JOHN RONALD was a boy who loved horses.
And trees. And strange sounding words.

1

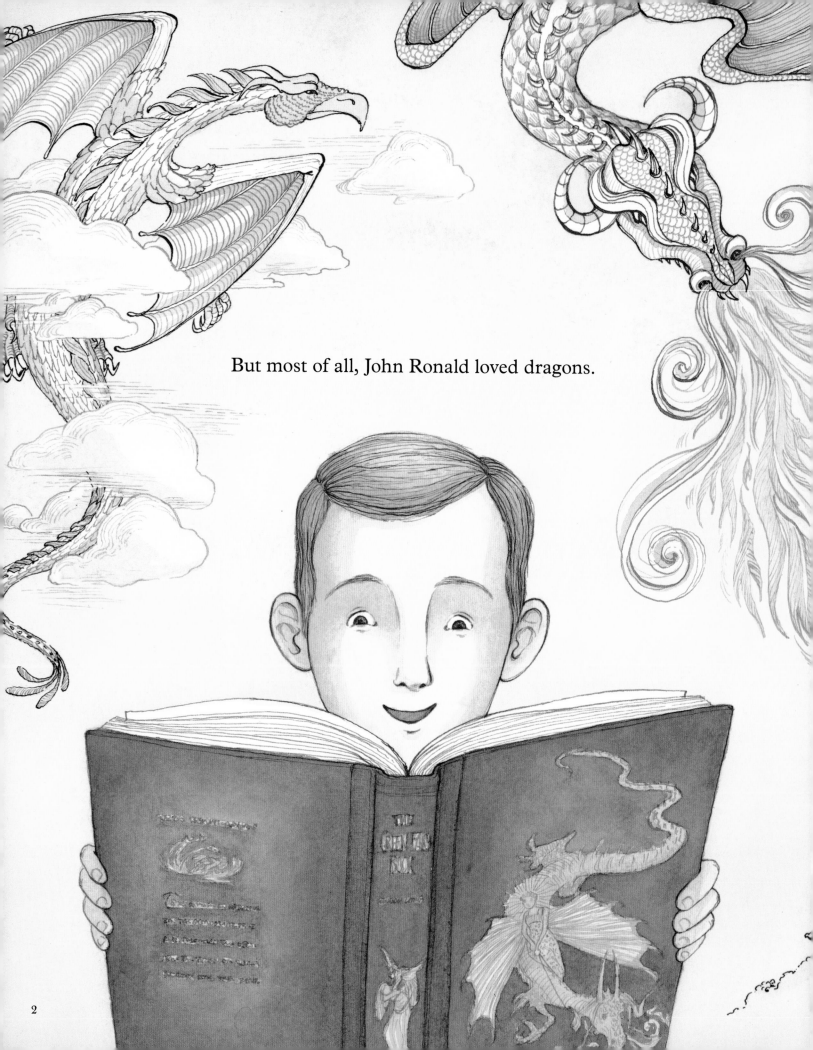

But most of all, John Ronald loved dragons.

Dragons that flew through the clouds. Dragons that breathed sizzling flames. Dragons that tied themselves in knots. Dragons that wore shining scales. And dragons that guarded ancient treasure.

John Ronald fed sugar cubes to the milkman's horse. He swung from the branches of beech trees with his little brother.

4

His mother read him stories about brave knights who battled dragons. But in safe Sarehole, a small town in Britain's Midlands, no actual dragons flew through the clouds—only geese and sometimes a hawk.

At school John Ronald made good friends. The boys
held secret parties in the library with tea and biscuits. The
librarian scolded them for dropping crumbs on her books.

6

They acted in plays, and they played rugby. They sketched pictures and made jokes. But at school there were no dragons that breathed sizzling flames—only the headmaster who smoked a pipe.

On vacations from school, John Ronald visited his cousin, Mary. They made up their own language.

Dar fys ma vel gom co palt "Hoc
Pys go iskili far maino Woc?
Pro si go fys do roc de
Do cat ym maino bocte
De volt fact soc ma taimful gyroc!"

which meant: There was an old man who said "How
Can I possibly carry my cow?
For if I was to ask it
To get in my basket
It would make such a terrible row."

The grown-ups shrugged their shoulders. At his cousin's house there were no dragons tied up in knots—only John Ronald and Mary who tied themselves in knots laughing at their private language.

9

Then John Ronald's mother died. He and his brother moved in with their aunt. She didn't like boys, and her house was cold and lonely.

At night John Ronald
dreamed of exploring a
steamy dragon's den,

but in the morning when he walked into his aunt's kitchen, nothing warmed the room—only a thin wisp of steam rose from his lumpy oatmeal.

13

On the way from his aunt's house to school, John Ronald stopped at the church. There he helped Father Francis perform the morning mass. He carried a cross up the aisle. He rang the altar bell.

Of course, he didn't find any dragons at the church—but he did find stillness, beauty, and peace.

After some time,
John Ronald moved
to a boarding house.
There he met a girl
with bright eyes and
shining black hair.

16

He fell in love and asked her to marry him, and she agreed. For a while, he forgot to look for dragons with shining scales. He only had eyes for Edith as she played scales on her piano.

All of a sudden the whole world went to war. John Ronald had to go too. He trudged through mud. He slept in a trench. He heard loud guns. For as far as he could see in any direction, the war had destroyed all the green trees.

He tried to shut out the noises of war by making up another imaginary language. It didn't work. It was then that he most needed dragons. But, of course, there were no dragons on the battlefield—only ugly machines belching flames.

When John Ronald came home, he got a job teaching at the University of Oxford. He gave lectures. He went to meetings. He tutored students. He graded many, many exams.

When he could escape from his work, he ate fish and chips at the pub with his friends. Sometimes they read each other stories they had written. But there were still no dragons guarding treasure—only silent gargoyles guarding buildings.

Then one day when John Ronald was
grading exams, he came to a blank page.

He wrote on the page,

In a hole in the ground
there lived a hobbit.

He didn't yet know what a hobbit
was. It wasn't a dragon, but he followed
it anyway.

On school holidays in winter when the fire was lit and the tea kettle was whistling, John Ronald told his children stories about the hobbit, who, by the way, he named Bilbo Baggins.

He gave Bilbo hairy feet. Bilbo lived in a cozy underground home in the Shire.

But most important of all,
Bilbo led John Ronald over the
Misty Mountains,

through the Mirkwood Forest,

and across the Long Lake to the base of the
Lonely Mountain.

There, at last, John Ronald
found his dragon.

And deep under the Lonely Mountain there still lives a dragon that flies through the clouds and breathes sizzling flames. A dragon that wears shining scales and guards ancient treasure.

A dragon named Smaug.

Author's Note

John Ronald Reuel Tolkien was born in South Africa in 1892. When John Ronald was three, his mother took him to England for a visit. While they were in England, his father died suddenly of rheumatic fever. Tolkien's mother was left to raise him and his younger brother on her own.

She settled in the small village of Sarehole near Birmingham. In Sarehole Tolkien first read "The Story of Sigurd" in Andrew Lang's *The Red Fairy Book* where he met the fearsome dragon Fafnir. He also fell in love with the strange Welsh words he saw written on passing train cars and made up imaginary languages with his cousin.

Tolkien's happy childhood was shattered when his mother died of diabetes. He was just twelve years old. At first he and his brother moved in with his aunt, the widow of his mother's younger brother. His mother had appointed a Catholic priest, Father Francis Morgan, to be his guardian, and Father Francis paid the aunt to take care of the boys. However, she offered the orphaned boys no affection. One day they returned from school to discover that she had burned their mother's belongings. Father Francis then moved them to a boarding house.

At King Edward's School in Birmingham, Tolkien's close circle of friends helped him to cope with the loneliness of being an orphan. They called themselves the TCBS, which stood for the Tea Club and Barrovian Society. The name came from their drinking tea at Barrow's Stores and also from holding illicit tea parties in the school library.

Tolkien met the love of his life, Edith Bratt, at the boarding house where he lived in Birmingham. She was an orphan like him. Father Francis worried that she would distract Tolkien from his studies. After all, he could not attend university unless he won a scholarship. Father Francis forbade Tolkien to see Edith or write her for two years. Tolkien obeyed, but when the two years were up, he immediately proposed. They married before he left for France to fight in the First World War.

As a member of the Lancashire Fusiliers, Tolkien fought in the Battle of the Somme, where Britain lost over 400,000 men. Two of his closest friends from the TCBS died there.

After the war, Tolkien became a renowned professor of Anglo-Saxon at Oxford University. He met with other literary friends, including C. S. Lewis, at pubs around Oxford. They called their informal society the Inklings.

Tolkien and his wife had four children. When I visited Oxford, I was delighted to discover that Tolkien sent his sons to the Dragon School, a progressive school in North Oxford that is still in existence.

In 1936 Tolkien began writing *The Hobbit* to read to his children during winter break. When he submitted it to the publisher George Allen and Unwin, Stanley Unwin gave the manuscript to his ten-year-old son, Rainor, to review. Rainor wrote, "This book with the help of maps does not need any illustrations. It is good and should appeal to all children between the ages of 5 and 7." *The Hobbit* was published in 1937. Prompted by its worldwide success, Tolkien proceeded to write The Lord of the Rings trilogy.

In writing a biography of J. R. R. Tolkien for children, I wanted to capture the life of his imagination. After all, he lived quietly. It was in his imagination that he traveled far and took extraordinary risks. In spite of the international success he garnered from his writing, Tolkien remained in England until his death in 1973. He maintained that he was, except for his size, in every way a hobbit.

Illustrator's Note

J. R. R. Tolkien was against the suggestion that his work was allegorical—what he put into his writing wasn't meant to directly represent the stuff of his life experience—but as I immersed myself in the real and imagined worlds of Tolkien it became clear to me that his surroundings, interests, and experiences clearly permeate his creative landscapes. One cannot help but see the Shire in the English countryside, Mirkwood Forest in Moseley Bog, or Rivendell in the buildings of Oxford.

I approached the artwork with the intent of balancing history and fantasy. To bring in the fantasy element, dragons and dragon-like shapes appear throughout the book. I think pointing each one out would take the fun out of finding them, so I will leave that up to the reader. But some historical details in the artwork that are not included in the written text are worth noting:

1 The village of Sarehole inspired Tolkien's Shire. In the background are the Sarehole Mill and pond. I show the waterwheel on the outside of the building, but the actual wheel is hidden from view inside the mill.

2–3 Here you see Andrew Lang's *The Green Fairy Book*, decorated with a beautiful golden dragon. In the page that follows, Tolkien's mother is reading out of his favorite Lang book, *The Red Fairy Book*.

4–5 Childhood recollections of Tolkien and his brother, Hilary, include playing in Sarehole village and getting chased off by the miller and a local farmer (both shown in silhouette), who they nicknamed the White Ogre and the Black Ogre. To the right of Sarehole Mill is a weeping willow—a favorite tree of Tolkien's that he found cut down one day, which affected him long after.

10 Close to Tolkien's aunt's house stands Edgbaston's Waterworks tower and the Perrott's Folly tower, which are thought to have inspired the title of The Lord Of The Rings second volume, *The Two Towers*. John Ronald and Hilary's luggage include a trunk labeled A. R. Tolkien, which references Tolkien's only memory of his father, Arthur Tolkien, painting his own name on a family trunk before John Ronald left South Africa as a three-year-old.

13 Tolkien's aunt burns his mother's letters in the kitchen stove.

16 Edith's window was directly below John Ronald's window at the boarding house where they shared long talks until dawn. In the background is the clock at Five Ways junction. The bikes represent an incident when John Ronald and Edith snuck off for a country bike ride together after being forbidden to see each other (and got caught).

17 Edith is playing an upright Tolkien piano, which references Tolkien's grandfather settling in Birmingham as a piano maker. Before they were separated for two years, they exchanged secret birthday gifts: a fountain pen for his nineteenth, and a watch for her twenty-first.

18–19 John Ronald grew a mustache during war time, but I chose to omit this detail to keep him recognizable as he ages through the story. During this time, Tolkien had been developing what would become his elvish language, Quenya. The poppies above John Ronald represent his coming upon a field of poppies amidst the war fields on a walk with T.C.B.S. friend, G. B. Smith. Smith died at the Somme shortly after encouraging Tolkien to start work on his mythology.

20 I used some forced perspective in this scene to include famous Oxford landmarks: the Bridge of Sighs, the Sheldonian Theatre, and the Bodleian Library.

21 This view of The Eagle and Child pub is changed to fit the composition. In reality the pub is attached to a building on its left side and the sign is over the front door.

22–23 Tolkien used a Hammond typewriter and dip pen for his writing. Book covers in this scene include: *The Story of King Arthur, Sir Gawain & The Green Knight, Beowulf,* and a set of Oxford English Dictionaries, to which Tolkien contributed work in 1919–1920.

24 The fabric on Tolkien's chair is inspired by patterns of the artist William Morris, an artistic influence of Tolkien's time.

A Catalog of Tolkien's Dragons

There were two important dragons from legend that influenced Tolkien.

1. **Fafnir**—Fafnir was the first mythical dragon that ignited Tolkien's imagination. He read about him in "The Story of Sigurd" in Andrew Lang's *The Red Fairy Book*.
2. **The Beowulf Dragon**—Tolkien was an Anglo-Saxon scholar and studied and wrote about the poem *Beowulf*. He considered the dragon in *Beowulf* to be one of the most important dragons in Western mythology.

Tolkien created several dragons, who make appearances in his stories. The four most important are listed below. As you can see, he took great care in naming them.

1. **Smaug**—Smaug is the name of the dragon in *The Hobbit*. He lives underneath the Lonely Mountain and his name comes from the primitive Germanic verb *Smugan*, which means to squeeze through a hole.
2. **Chrysophylax**—The dragon in the short book *Farmer Giles of Ham* is named Chrysophylax Dives, which means "rich keeper of gold." *Chrysophylax* comes from the Greek for *gold-keeper* and *dives* comes from the Latin for *rich*.
3. **Glaurung**—Glaurung is the dragon in *The Children of Hurin*. He is known as the father of dragons. The first part of his name, *glaur*, means *golden* in Tolkien's invented language of Sindarin. The second part of his name, *ung*, means *gloom*.
4. **Ancalagon the Black**—Ancalagon the Black is in *The Silmarillion* and is also mentioned briefly in the second chapter of *The Fellowship of the Ring*. Again his name comes from Tolkien's invented language of Sindarin, and it means *rushing jaws*.

Quotes from Tolkien's Scholarly Writing on Dragons

"I desired dragons with a profound desire. Of course, I in my timid body did not wish to have them in the neighborhood, intruding into my relatively safe world, in which it was, for instance, possible to read stories in peace of mind, free from fear. But the world that contained even the imagination of Fafnir was richer and more beautiful, at whatever cost of peril."

—"On Fairy-Stories"

"And dragons, real dragons, essential both to the machinery and the ideas of a poem or tale, are actually rare . . . He [the Beowulf poet] esteemed dragons, as rare as they are dire, as some do still. He liked them—as a poet, not as a sober zoologist; and he had good reason."

—*"Beowulf*: The Monsters and the Critics"

"A serpent creature, but with four legs and claws; his neck varied in length but had a hideous head with long jaws and teeth or snake tongue. He was usually heavily armoured especially on his head and back and flanks. Nonetheless he was pretty bendable (up and down or sideways), and could even tie himself in knots on occasion, and had a long powerful tail . . . Some had wings . . . A respectable dragon should be 20 ft or more."

—unpublished lecture on dragons that Tolkien gave to children at the Museum of Natural History, Oxford, 1938

Bibliography

Carpenter, Humphrey. *J. R. R. Tolkien: A Biography.* Boston: Houghton Mifflin, 2000.

Carpenter, Humphrey. *The Inklings: C. S. Lewis, J. R. R. Tolkien, Charles William, and Their Friends.* Boston: Houghton Mifflin, 1979.

Carpenter, Humphrey (Ed.) and Christopher Tolkien. *The Letters of J. R. R. Tolkien.* Boston: Houghton Mifflin, 2000.

Garth, John. *Tolkien and the Great War: The Threshold of Middle-earth.* Boston: Houghton Mifflin, 2003.

Hammond, Wayne G. and Christina Scull. *J. R. R. Tolkien: Artist and Illustrator.* Boston: Houghton Mifflin, 1995.

Poe, Harry Lee. *The Inklings of Oxford: C. S. Lewis, J. R. R. Tolkien, and Their Friends.* Grand Rapids, Michigan: Zondervan, 2009.

Tolkien, J. R. R. "On Fairy-Stories." *The Tolkien Reader: Stories, Poems, and Commentaries by the Author of The Hobbit and The Lord of the Rings.* New York: Ballantine, 1966.

Tolkien, J. R. R. *The Monsters and the Critics and Other Essays.* Boston: Houghton Mifflin, 1984.